JAZZ PIANO SOLOS VOLUME 40

# charlie parker

Arranged by Brent Edstrom

T0117633

## contents


2 APRIL IN PARIS
7 AU PRIVAVE
12 BILLIE'S BOUNCE (BILL'S BOUNCE)
22 BLOOMDIDO
17 CONFIRMATION
26 DEWEY SQUARE
31 DONNA LEE
36 THE GYPSY
44 JUST FRIENDS
50 LOVER MAN (OH, WHERE CAN YOU BE?)
39 MOOSE THE MOOCHE
54 MY LITTLE SUEDE SHOES
59 NOW'S THE TIME
64 ORNITHOLOGY
69 OUT OF NOWHERE
76 PARKER'S MOOD
79 RELAXIN' AT THE CAMARILLO
84 SCRAPPLE FROM THE APPLE
89 SUMMERTIME
92 YARDBIRD SUITE


Cover photo: William P. Gottlieb Collection/Library of Congress

ISBN 978-1-4950-3082-6

HAL•LEONARD® CORPORATION
7777 W. BLUEMOUND RD. P.O. BOX 13819 MILWAUKEE, WI 53213

For all works contained herein:
Unauthorized copying, arranging, adapting, recording, Internet posting, public performance, or other distribution of the printed music in this publication is an infringement of copyright. Infringers are liable under the law.

Visit Hal Leonard Online at
**www.halleonard.com**

# APRIL IN PARIS

Words by E.Y. "YIP" HARBURG
Music by VERNON DUKE

Copyright © 1932 by Kay Duke Music and Glocca Morra Music LLC
Copyright Renewed
This arrangement Copyright © 2016 by Kay Duke Music and Glocca Morra Music LLC
All Rights for Kay Duke Music Administered by Universal Music Corp.
All Rights for Glocca Morra Music LLC Administered by Shapiro, Bernstein & Co., Inc.
International Copyright Secured All Rights Reserved

Swing 8ths
E♭maj13
E♭maj7
C♭maj9
B♭maj9
Gm7
Gm7/F
Em7♭5
A9
Straight 8ths
D7
G7♭9
Swing 8ths
Cm7
E♭dim7
B♭6/D
E7♯11
E♭dim7
B♭/D Cm7
B♭
Gm9
Am11♭5
D7
Gm7
Gm7/F
Em7♭5
A7
Dmaj9
F7♯5
A♭9/F
A6/F
B♭6/F

Dm7♭5
A♭9
G9♯5
G13
f
Straight 8ths
C13
B9
C9
F9
Gm6
mp
E♭m(maj7)
N.C.
mf
G7♯5(♭9)
G13♭9
G9
D♭13
G13
Swing 8ths
B♭13/C
F♯dim7/G
C6/G
C6
Dm7♭5
E♭m7/G
Dm7/G
f

G13
G13♭9
Cmaj9
Cdim(maj7)/G
C6/G
C6/9
Gm7
Gm11
C9
F6
Em7
Am7
Am7/G
F♯m7♭5
B7♭9
E9
A9
F6
Fdim7
C(add2)/E
E♭dim7
G7♭9/D
Dm7♭5/G
C6
Am7

Bm11♭5
E7♭9
Am
Am7/G
F♯m7♭5
B7♯5
Emaj7
G13sus
G13
Dm7♭5/G
C6/G
mf
cresc.
Em7♭5
A♭13
A13
D9
Straight 8ths
G9sus
G7♭9
Cmaj7
Dm11
Dm9
D♭maj7
ff
Cmaj9
B6/C
C6

# AU PRIVAVE

By CHARLIE PARKER

Copyright © 1956 (Renewed 1984) Atlantic Music Corp.
This arrangement Copyright © 2016 Atlantic Music Corp.
International Copyright Secured All Rights Reserved

2.
Gm9
C7
F6
Gm7
C7
Solo based on ones by Charlie Parker and Dizzy Gillespie
F7
Cm7
F7
B♭9
B♭m6
Fmaj7
Gm7
Am7
D7♭9
Gm9
C7
Fmaj7
Gm7
C7
F
Gm7
C7

F
Cm7
F7
B♭7
Bdim7
F6
Gm7
E♭9
D9
Gm7
C7
Gm7
C7♭9
C9
F
Cm7
C7
3
F7
B7♯11
B♭7
3
F
D♭7
Cm7
F7
B♭9

F
Gm7
Am7
D7
Gm7
D♭7
C7♭9
3
F
Gm7
C13
F6/9
B♭9
Bdim7
F/C
F7♯11
B♭9
F
Gm7
Am7
D7♭9
Gm7
C9
F
D7♯9

Gm7
C7
F
B♭
Bdim
F
Cm7
F7
B♭7
Fmaj7
Gm7
Am7
A♭m7
Gm7
D.C. al Coda
C7
F7♯11
Gm7
C9
CODA
Gm9
Fmaj7

# BILLIE'S BOUNCE
## (Bill's Bounce)

**Moderate Swing**

By CHARLIE PARKER

Copyright © 1945 (Renewed 1973) Atlantic Music Corp.
This arrangement Copyright © 2016 Atlantic Music Corp.
All Rights for the World excluding the U.S. Controlled and Administered by Screen Gems-EMI Music Inc.
International Copyright Secured All Rights Reserved

To Coda
Gm7
A♭7♯11
Gm7
C7
Am7
A♭13♯11
1.
Gm7
C9sus
2.
Gm7
C9sus
F
F/A
Solo based on one by Charlie Parker
B♭7
Bdim7
F/C
F13
Cm7
F13
B♭9
F
B♭9
Am7
A♭m7
Gm7
D♭7
C7

Am7
D9
G13
G♭13♯9
F
F7
F7♯11
B♭7
B♭9
F
Gm
A7
D7
Gm7
C7
F
D7♭9
Gm7
C7sus
f
F7
B♭
F

F9
B♭9
F
Gm

Am7
D7♭9
Gm
C7

F
Gm
C9
F13
B7
B♭7
F13

G♭9♯11
Cm7
F13
B13
B♭7

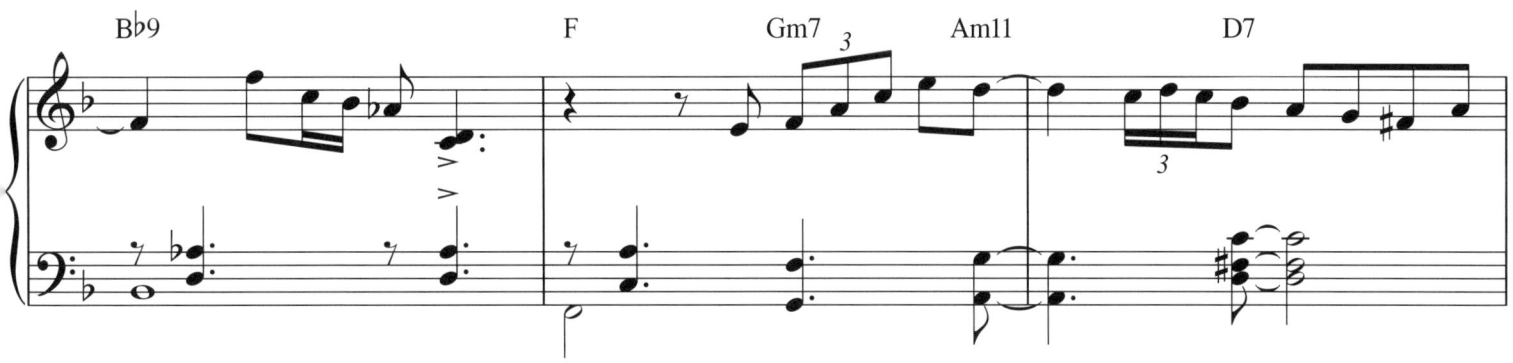
B♭9
F
Gm7
Am11
D7

Gm7
F♯7♯5
Gm7
C13
Am7
A♭7

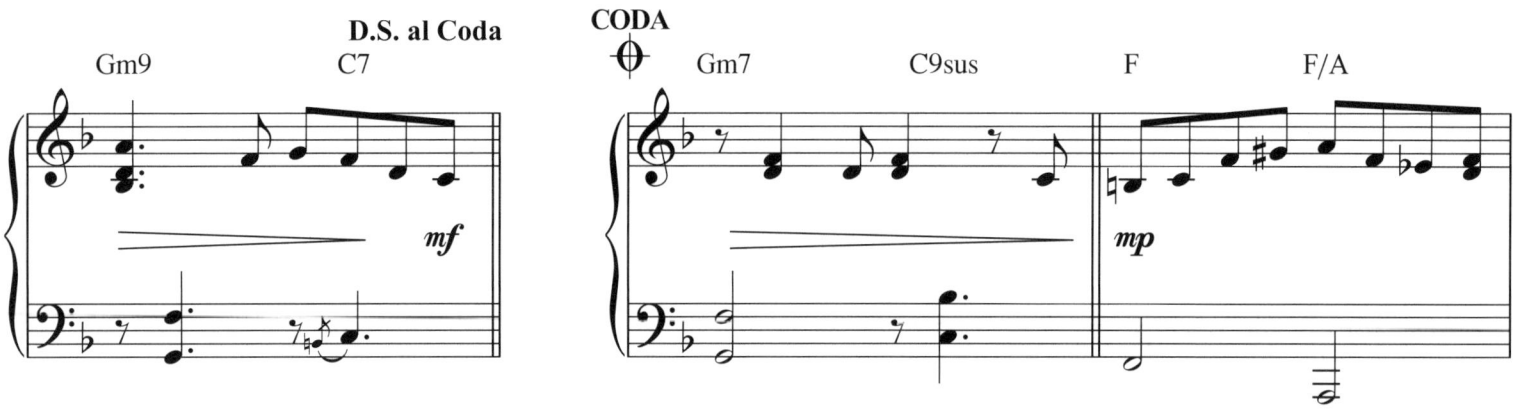
D.S. al Coda
CODA
Gm9
C7
mf
Gm7
C9sus
F
F/A
mp

B♭
Bdim7
F/C
F/B♭
F/A
F(♯5)
B9♯11
B♭9

F/C
Gm/B♭
Am7
D7♭9

Gm7
mf
C7sus
F
B♭
Bdim
F6/C
F7♯11

# CONFIRMATION

By CHARLIE PARKER

Copyright © 1946 (Renewed 1974) Atlantic Music Corp.
This arrangement Copyright © 2016 Atlantic Music Corp.
International Copyright Secured All Rights Reserved

F
Em7♭5
A7
Dm
Cm7
F7
B♭7
E♭7
D7
Gm7
C7
F/C
Cm7
Cm(maj7)
f
Cm7
B13
B♭maj7
F9♯5
B♭6/9
E♭m7
A♭9
A♭7♯5
D♭maj9
D♭6/9

Gm7♭5
C7♯5(♭9)
F6
mf
Em7♭5
A7
Dm
Cm7
F7
B♭9
To Coda
E♭7
D7
Gm7
C13
F/C
F
F6
Em7♭5
A7♭9
Dm
G9
Solo based on one by Charlie Parker
Cm7
F7
B♭9
Am7
A♭7♭9

G9
C7♯5
Fmaj7
F6
Em7♭5
A9sus
A7
Dm
D♭7
Cm7
F7
B♭6
E♭7
D7♭9
Gm7
C7
F
Cm7
F7
f
B♭6
Cm7
Dm7
Cm7
E♭m7

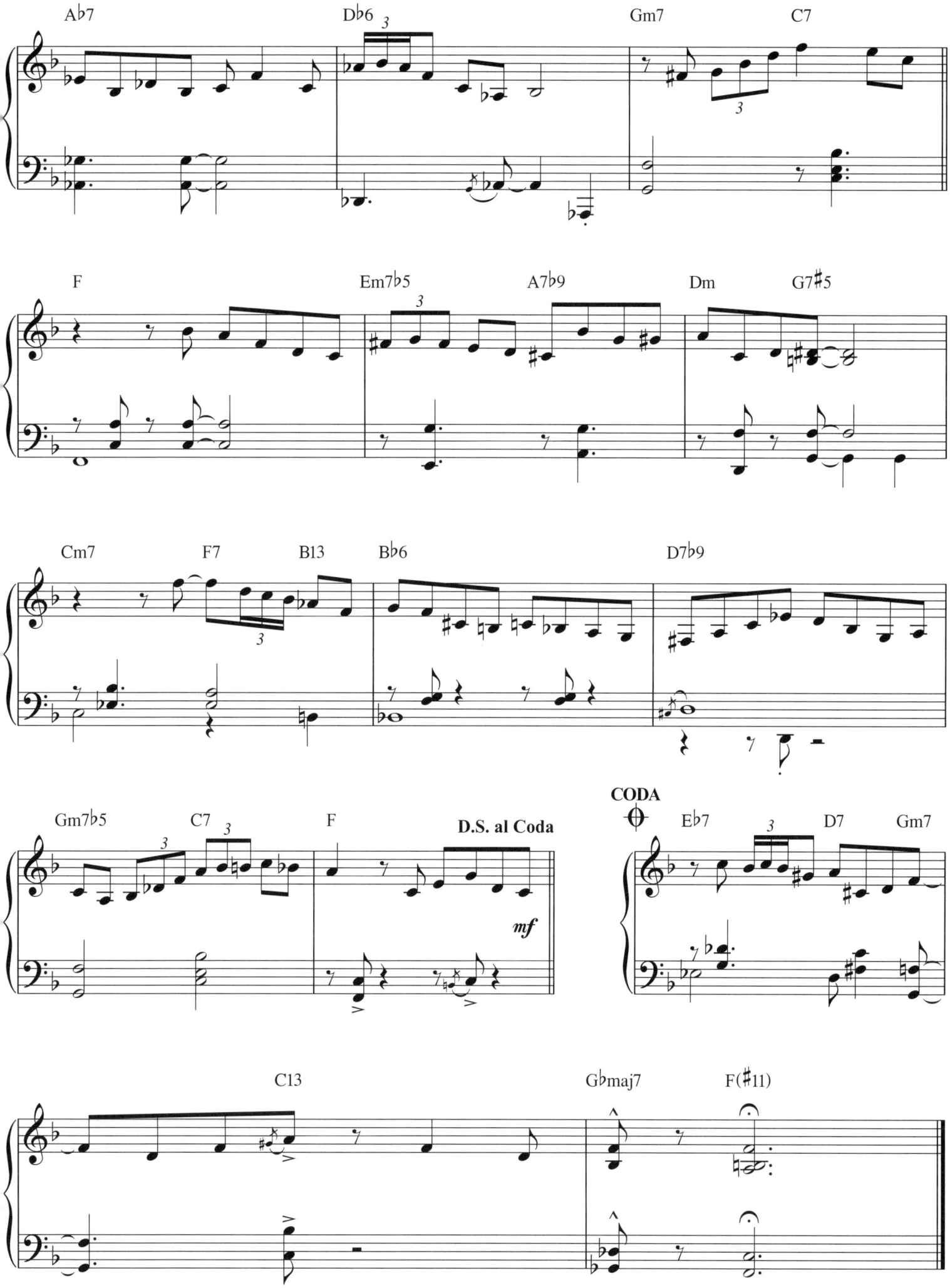
A♭7
D♭6
Gm7
C7
F
Em7♭5
A7♭9
Dm
G7♯5
Cm7
F7
B13
B♭6
D7♭9
Gm7♭5
C7
F
D.S. al Coda
mf
CODA
E♭7
D7
Gm7
C13
G♭maj7
F(♯11)

# BLOOMDIDO

By CHARLIE PARKER

Copyright © 1953 (Renewed 1981) Atlantic Music Corp.
This arrangement Copyright © 2016 Atlantic Music Corp.
International Copyright Secured All Rights Reserved

E♭
E♭m7
B♭
Cm
C♯m7
F♯7
Cm7
F7♭9
B♭
B♭6
E♭maj7
B♭/F
B♭7
E♭
E♭m7

C♯m7
F♯7
Cm7
F7♭9
To Coda
B♭
B♭7
Solo based on one by
Thelonious Monk
E♭7
B♭7
E♭7
B♭maj7
Dm7
C♯m7
Cm7
F7

F7
B♭
f
E♭
Edim
B♭/F
B♭7
E♭
B♭
Dm
D♭m
Cm
F
B♭6
D.S. al Coda
CODA
B9♯11
N.C./B♭
gliss.

# DEWEY SQUARE

By CHARLIE PARKER

Copyright © 1958 (Renewed 1986) Atlantic Music Corp.
This arrangement Copyright © 2016 Atlantic Music Corp.
International Copyright Secured All Rights Reserved

F9♯11
B♭7
Gm7
C7♭9
B♭9sus
B♭13
E♭maj7
A♭m7
D♭9
Gm7♭5
C9
3
F9♯11
B♭7
B7♯11
B♭7
E♭maj7
B♭m7
E♭9♯5
A♭maj7
A♭m7
D♭7
E♭maj9
Gm7
C7♭9

F7
F♯m7♭5
B7
B♭7♯5
B♭7
E♭maj9
A♭m7
D♭9
Gm7♭5
C9
F9♯11
B♭7
E♭(add2)
E♭maj9
A♭m7
D♭7
mf
Solo based on one by Charlie Parker
E♭(add2)
C7
F7
B♭7♯5

Gm7
C7
Fm7
B♭7
E9♯11
E♭maj9
A♭m7
D♭7
Gm7
C7
F7
B♭9
E♭maj7
B♭7♭9
E♭6
A♭maj7
D♭7
E♭maj9
C7
F13
Fm7

B♭7♯5
E♭maj9
D♭7
E♭
C7♯5
F9
B♭7
E♭
Fm7
B♭7♭9
f
E♭maj9
A♭m7
D♭9
Gm7♭5
C9
F9♯11
Fm7
B♭7
E♭maj7
E♭maj9

# DONNA LEE

By CHARLIE PARKER

Copyright © 1947 (Renewed 1975) Atlantic Music Corp.
This arrangement Copyright © 2016 Atlantic Music Corp.
All Rights for the World excluding the U.S. Controlled and Administered by Screen Gems-EMI Music Inc.
International Copyright Secured All Rights Reserved

D♭6/9
D♭m9
G♭13
A♭maj7
F7
B7♯11
B♭7
Fm7
B♭7♯11
B♭m7
E♭7
E♭7♭9
A♭maj7
F7
B♭7
C7
Gm7♭5
C7
Fm6

Gm11b5
C7b5(b9)
Gb7#11
Fm(add9)
C7
Gb7
Fm
3
Bb7b9
Bdim7
Cm7
F7
To Coda
Bbm7
Eb13
Ab/Eb
Solo based on one by Charlie Parker
Abmaj13
Gb9
F9
Bb7
B9
Bb9
Bbm7
3
Eb7
A7b5

A♭maj13
E♭m7
A♭13
D♭6
3
D♭m7
G♭7
A♭maj7
F7
B7
B♭7
3
B7
B♭7
B♭m7
E♭7
A7♭9
A♭maj13
F7♭9
B♭9
B13
B♭13
Gm7♭5
3

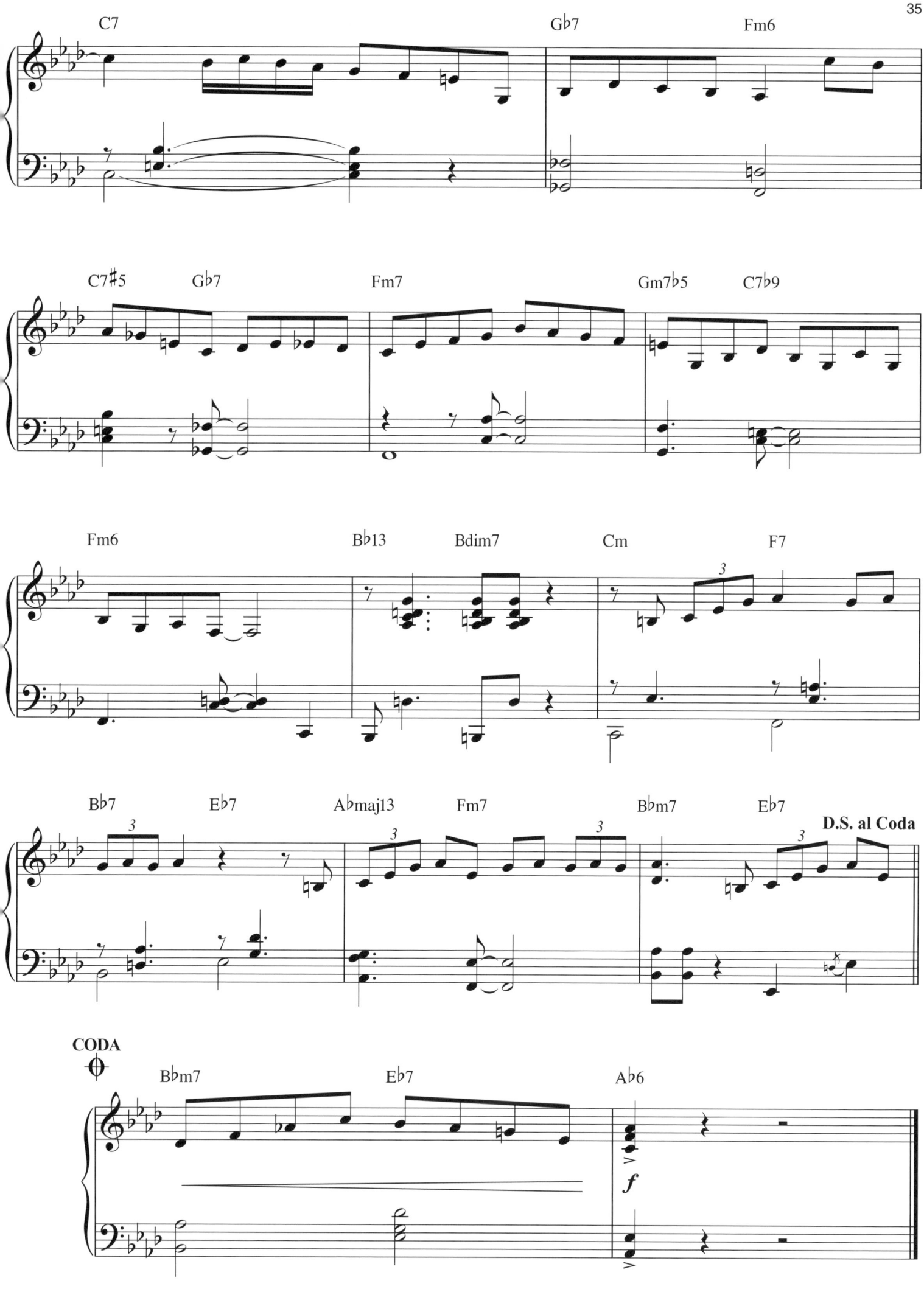
C7
G♭7
Fm6
C7♯5
G♭7
Fm7
Gm7♭5
C7♭9
Fm6
B♭13
Bdim7
Cm
F7
B♭7
E♭7
A♭maj13
Fm7
B♭m7
E♭7
D.S. al Coda
CODA
B♭m7
E♭7
A♭6
f

# THE GYPSY

Words and Music by
BILLY REID

Copyright © 1945 UNIVERSAL MUSIC CORP. and PETER MAURICE MUSIC CO. LTD.
Copyright Renewed
This arrangement Copyright © 2016 UNIVERSAL MUSIC CORP. and PETER MAURICE MUSIC CO. LTD.
All Rights for the U.S. and Canada Controlled and Administered by UNIVERSAL MUSIC CORP.
All Rights Reserved Used by Permission

E♭m11
A♭7
D♭maj7
E♭m7
C(add2)/E
Fm7
B9
B♭9♯5
E7
E♭9
B♭m9
E♭9♯11
B♭m11
A7♭5
E♭m7
A♭13
E♭m7
D7♯9
D♭6/9
G♭m7
D♭(add2)
Fm11
E7♯11
E♭m9
D7♭9
f
D♭maj7
Fm7
Em7
E♭m9
D7♭9
D♭maj9
D♭6/9

Fm
Fm(♯5)
Fm
E♭m7

A♭9sus
D7♯9
D♭maj9
E♭m7
Fm7
B♭9♯5
mf

To Coda
E♭9
B♭m7/F
E♭13♭5(♭9)
A7♭9
E♭m7
A♭13

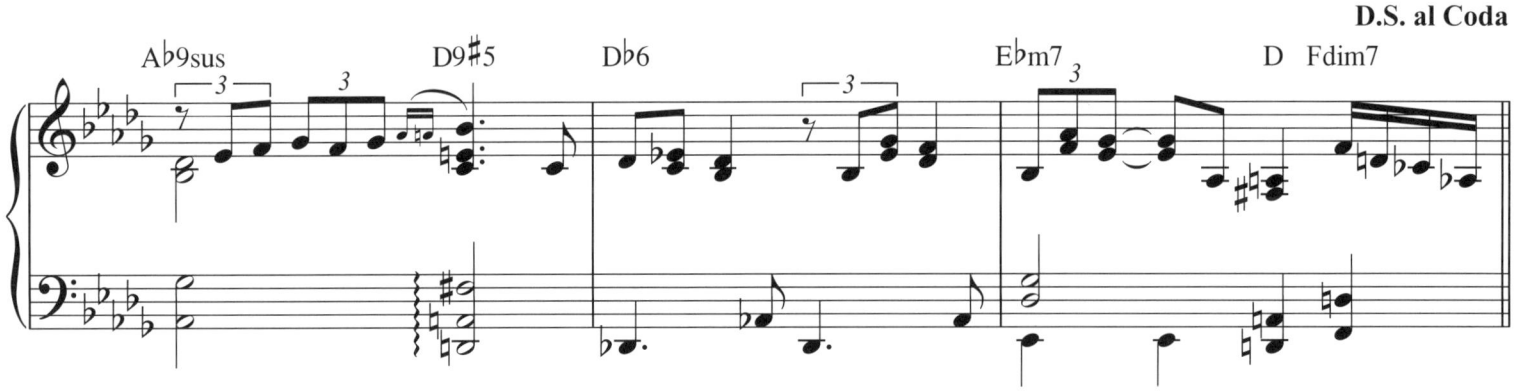
D.S. al Coda
A♭9sus
D9♯5
D♭6
E♭m7
D
Fdim7

CODA
A♭9sus
D9♭5(♯5)
Freely
D♭maj13

# MOOSE THE MOOCHE

By CHARLIE PARKER

Copyright © 1946 (Renewed 1974) Atlantic Music Corp.
This arrangement Copyright © 2016 Atlantic Music Corp.
International Copyright Secured All Rights Reserved

Cm7
F7
B♭6
Gm7
Cm7
Cm7♭5/F
B♭6
Gm7
Cm7
F7
Fm7
B♭7♭9
E♭
E♭m7
B♭/F
D7
f
Am7
D7
Dm7
G13
Gm7
C9
Cm7
F7

B♭6 Gm7 Cm7 F7 B♭6 Gm7 Cm7 F7
mf
Fm7 B♭7 E♭ Edim7 B♭/F
To Coda
B♭6 Gm7 Cm7♭5 F7
Solo based on one by Charlie Parker
B♭6/D Gm7 Cm7 F7 B♭6 B♭7 E♭6 E♭m6
B♭/F G♭7 F7 B♭6 Gm7 Cm7

F7
Dm7
G7
Cm7
F7
B♭7
E♭6
E♭m
B♭/F
B♭7♯11
Am9
D13♯11
f
G13
C7
Gm7
C7
F7

B♭6
Bdim7
Cm7
F7
Dm7
D♭m7
Cm7
F7
B♭7
E♭
Edim7
B♭/F
F7♭9
D.S. al Coda
CODA
B♭
mp
p
ff

# JUST FRIENDS

Lyrics by SAM M. LEWIS
Music by JOHN KLENNER

© 1931 (Renewed) METRO-GOLDWYN-MAYER, INC.
This arrangement © 2016 METRO-GOLDWYN-MAYER, INC.
All Rights Controlled by EMI ROBBINS CATALOG INC. (Publishing) and ALFRED MUSIC (Print)
All Rights Reserved Used by Permission

A♭maj7
A♭6
A♭13
A♭7♯5
Swing 8ths
D♭maj9
3
G♭9
A♭maj9
A♭6
3
E7
B♭m7
E♭9
A♭maj7

B♭7
E♭13sus
A♭13
A♭9♯5
D♭maj9
D♭maj7
D♭6/9
G♭9
A♭maj9
B♭m7
A♭maj9
E7
E9
B♭m7
E♭9
Gm7♭5
C7♭9
Fm7
B♭13
E♭7

A♭6
D♭13
D♭9♯11
Fm7
E7♯9
E♭6/9
f
A♭9
B♭maj7
G♭9
Cm7

F13
G♭7
F7
B♭6/9
C7
F7sus
G♭7
F7
B♭7♯5
E♭
A♭m7
A♭7
B♭6
D♭m7
G♭13
D♭m7
G♭7
Cm7

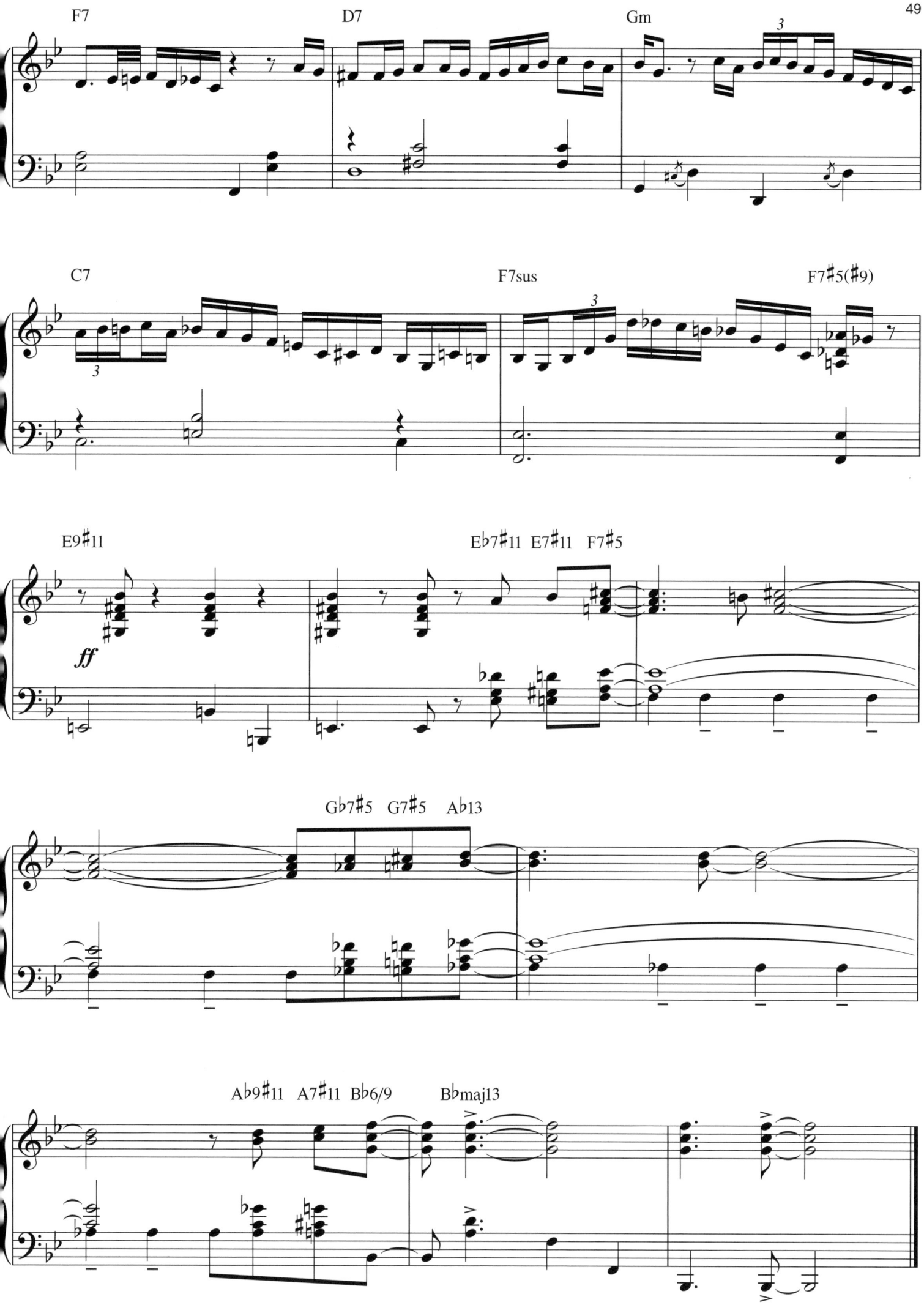
F7
D7
Gm
C7
F7sus
F7♯5(♯9)
E9♯11
ff
E♭7♯11 E7♯11 F7♯5
G♭7♯5 G7♯5 A♭13
A♭9♯11 A7♯11 B♭6/9
B♭maj13

# LOVER MAN
## (Oh, Where Can You Be?)

Words and Music by JIMMY DAVIS,
ROGER RAMIREZ and JIMMY SHERMAN

Copyright © 1941, 1942 UNIVERSAL MUSIC CORP.
Copyright Renewed
This arrangement Copyright © 2016 UNIVERSAL MUSIC CORP.
All Rights Reserved Used by Permission

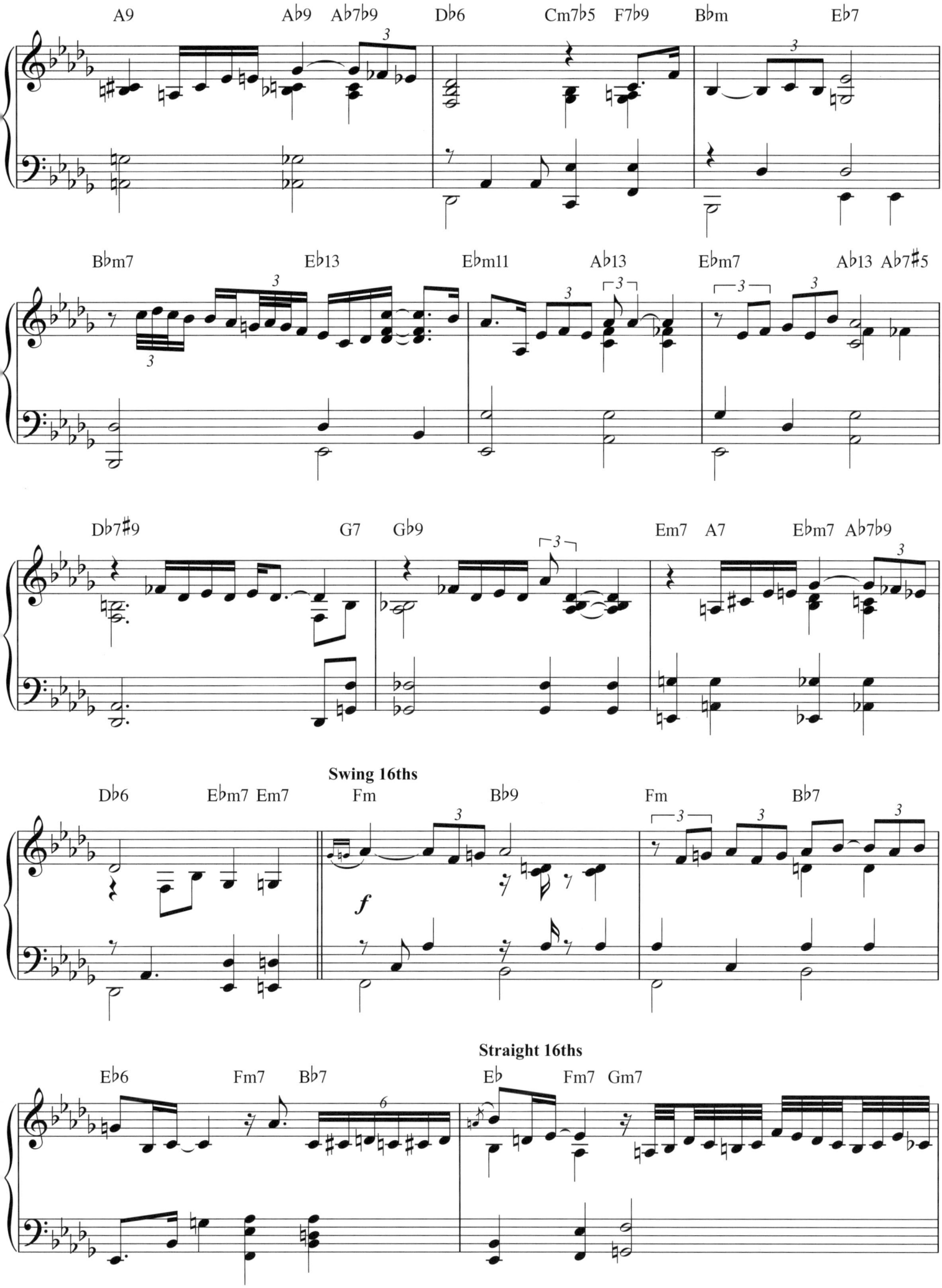
A9
A♭9
A♭7♭9
D♭6
Cm7♭5
F7♭9
B♭m
E♭7
B♭m7
E♭13
E♭m11
A♭13
E♭m7
A♭13
A♭7♯5
D♭7♯9
G7
G♭9
Em7
A7
E♭m7
A♭7♭9
Swing 16ths
D♭6
E♭m7
Em7
Fm
B♭9
Fm
B♭7
f
Straight 16ths
E♭6
Fm7
B♭7
E♭
Fm7
Gm7

E♭m7
A♭9♯11
E♭m7
A♭7
D♭6
Cm7
F7♯5(♭9)
B♭m7
E♭7
mf
B♭m7
E♭
A9♭5
A♭9
E♭m11
A♭7sus
A♭13
A♭7♯5
D♭7♯9
G7
G♭7
A7
A♭7
D♭maj7
E♭m7
Em7
Fm7
B♭9
Fm(add9)
B♭9
f

E♭
Fm
B♭7
E♭
Fm7
Gm7
Fm7
E♭m7
A♭13♭9/E♭
E♭m7
A♭9
D♭maj9
Cm11
F7♯5
B♭m7
E♭7
B♭m7
E♭7
A9♭5
A♭9
E♭m11
mf
A♭9
E♭m11
A♭7
D♭7♯9
G7
G♭9
Playfully
A7
E♭m7
A♭7
N.C.
D7♯9
D♭
rit.
f
ff

# MY LITTLE SUEDE SHOES

By CHARLIE PARKER

Copyright © 1956 (Renewed 1984) Atlantic Music Corp.
This arrangement Copyright © 2016 Atlantic Music Corp.
International Copyright Secured All Rights Reserved

Fm7
B♭9sus
E♭maj7
G13♯9
C13
C7♯5(♯9)
Fm9
B♭9
E♭6
A♭
Gm7
C9
f
Fm7
B♭9sus
E♭maj7
A♭
Gm7
C9
Fm7
B♭9sus
E♭6
Fm7
B♭7sus
E♭maj7
Fm7
B♭9sus
E♭6

To Coda
Fm7
B♭9sus
E♭maj7
C13
C7♯5
Fm9
B♭9sus
E♭
mf
Fm11
B♭7♭9
Solo based on one by Charlie Parker
E♭maj9
Fm11
B♭7♯9
Gm7
C7♭9
Fm7
B♭7
G7♯9
C7♭9
Fm7
B♭7
E♭6
Fm11
B♭9
E♭
C7

Fm
B♭7
Gm7♭5
C7♯5
Fm7
B♭7
Gm7♭5
C7♭9
Fm7
B♭7♯5
E♭
E♭7
A♭
Gm7
C7
Fm7
B♭7♭9
E♭
E♭7
A♭
Gm7
C7
Fm
B♭9sus
E♭maj9

Fm7
B♭13♭9
E♭maj7
Fm7
B♭7
E♭/B♭
C7
Fm7
B♭7
D♭13
C7♯9
Fm7
B♭9sus
E♭6
D.S. al Coda
mf
CODA
Fm9
B♭9sus
E♭6/B♭
G7♯5(♯9)
C13
C7♯5(♭9)
Fm9
B♭9sus
E♭6/B♭
G7♯5(♯9)
C13
C7♯5(♭9)
Fm9
B♭13
E♭maj9
ff

# NOW'S THE TIME

By CHARLIE PARKER

**Bright Swing**

Copyright © 1945 (Renewed 1973) Atlantic Music Corp.
This arrangement Copyright © 2016 Atlantic Music Corp.
All Rights for the World excluding the U.S. Controlled and Administered by Screen Gems-EMI Music Inc.
International Copyright Secured All Rights Reserved

*Solo based on one by Charlie Parker*

B♭7
F7
D7♯5
Gm7
C7
F7
Gm7
C7♭5
F9
B♭7
F7
B♭7
B♭9

F7
Am7
D7♭9
Gm11
C7
F7
Gm7
C7
F7
B♭7
F7
B♭7
F7
Am7
D7♭9
Gm7

C7
F7
3
G
C7♯5
F7
mf
B♭7
F7
B♭7
Bdim7
F7
Gm7
3
C7
F7♯9
Freely
8va

# ORNITHOLOGY

By CHARLIE PARKER
and BENNIE HARRIS

Copyright © 1946 (Renewed 1974) Atlantic Music Corp.
This arrangement Copyright © 2016 Atlantic Music Corp.
International Copyright Secured All Rights Reserved

B♭7
E♭7
D7
To Coda
1.
Gm
Am7
D7
Gmaj13
Bm7
B♭9
Am9
A♭13
2.
Gm
Am7
D7
Bm7
B♭m7
p
Am7
D7
Bm7
B♭m7
Am9
D13♭9
mp
mf

Gmaj7
Am7
Bm7
Am7
Gm7
Solo based on one by Charlie Parker
C7
G♭7
F
Gm7
F6
Fm7
B♭7
E7
E♭7
D7
Gm/D
Am7
D7♯5(♭9)
Bm7
C7
B♭m7

Am7
A♭maj7
Gmaj7
Gm7
C7
Fmaj7
3
Fm7
B7
B♭7
3
E♭7
Am7
D7
G
Am7
D7

Bm7♭5
B♭7
Am7
A♭7
G

Am7
D13
D.S. al Coda

CODA
Gm

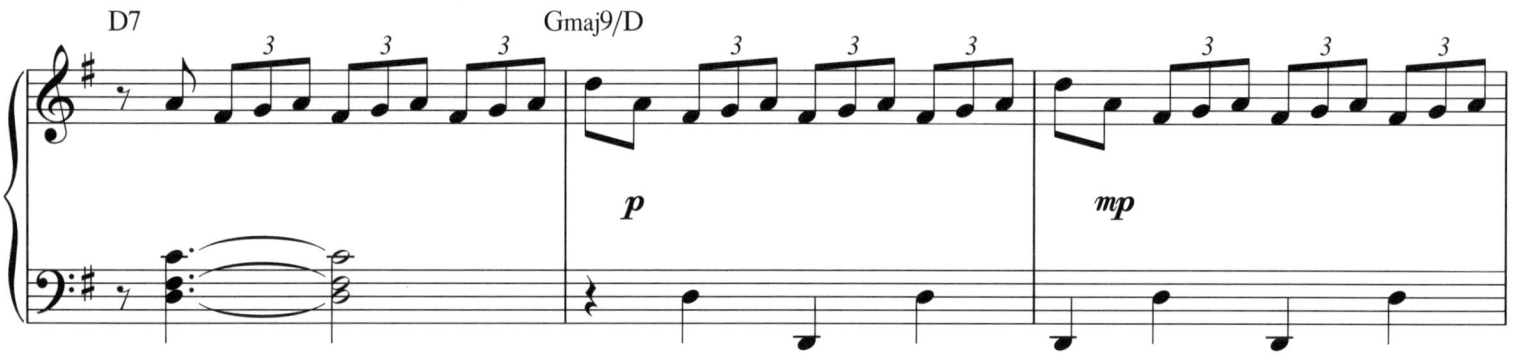
D7
Gmaj9/D
p
mp

G6/9
ff

# OUT OF NOWHERE

## from the Paramount Picture DUDE RANCH

Words by EDWARD HEYMAN
Music by JOHNNY GREEN

Copyright © 1931 Sony/ATV Music Publishing LLC
Copyright Renewed
This arrangement Copyright © 2016 Sony/ATV Music Publishing LLC
All Rights Administered by Sony/ATV Music Publishing LLC, 424 Church Street, Suite 1200, Nashville, TN 37219
International Copyright Secured All Rights Reserved

G6
Am7
A♯dim7
Bm7
Em7
Bm7
F7
E7
Am7
Bm7
E7
Am9
Am(maj9)
Am7
Am6
E♭9
Am11
D7
E♭7
D7
G
D7♭9
G6
B♭m7
E♭9
f

B♭m7
E♭9
Gmaj7
G6/9
Gmaj7
E9
Bm7
E7♯5
Am7
Bm7
E7
Am7
F7
Bm7
B♭dim7
Am11
A♭7
Am7/G
G
F7
B♭7
Gm9
cresc.

C13♯11
F
Gm
Am
F
ff
mf
A♭m7
D♭7
A♭m11
D♭7
F
Am
F
Am
D13
3
Gm
Am7
D7
Gm
D♭7
A♭m7

A♭m7/D♭
D♭7
G7
C7
C7♯5
Gm
G♭13
Fmaj9
Edim7 F6 Edim7 F6
f
Edim7
Bdim7 B♭9 F6
B♭9
D♭6 D♭9
C6
Gm7 C6
Gm7 C6
Gm7 Am7
B♭m6 C6
D9
D13
D9♯11
D7
mf
Gm

Am11♭5
D7♭9
Gm6/9
E♭9♯11
Am7
A♭dim7

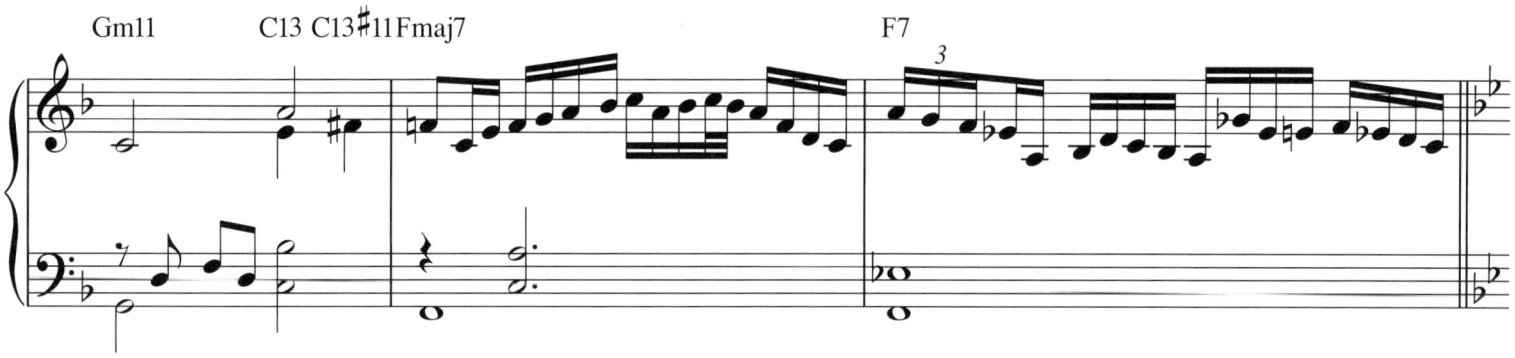
Gm11
C13 C13♯11
Fmaj7
F7

B♭maj7
Cm7
B♭6
D♭m7
G♭7

D♭m7
G♭9
B♭6
Cm7

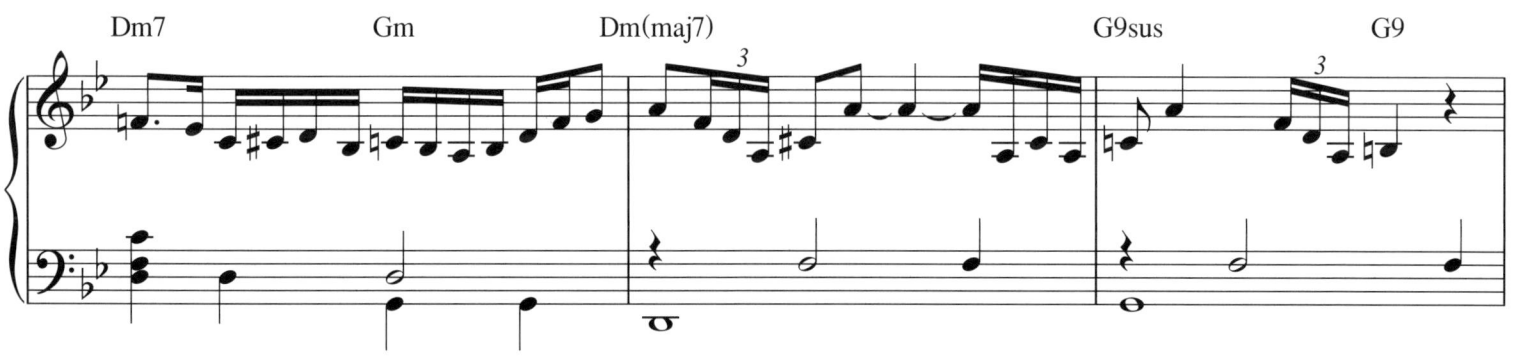
Dm7
Gm
Dm(maj7)
G9sus
G9

Cm7
Dm7♭5
G7♭9
Cm7
A♭7sus
A♭7
Dm7
D♭dim7
Cm7
B7♯9
B♭6
D♭m7
G♭13
Freely
B♭6/9
f

# PARKER'S MOOD

By CHARLIE PARKER

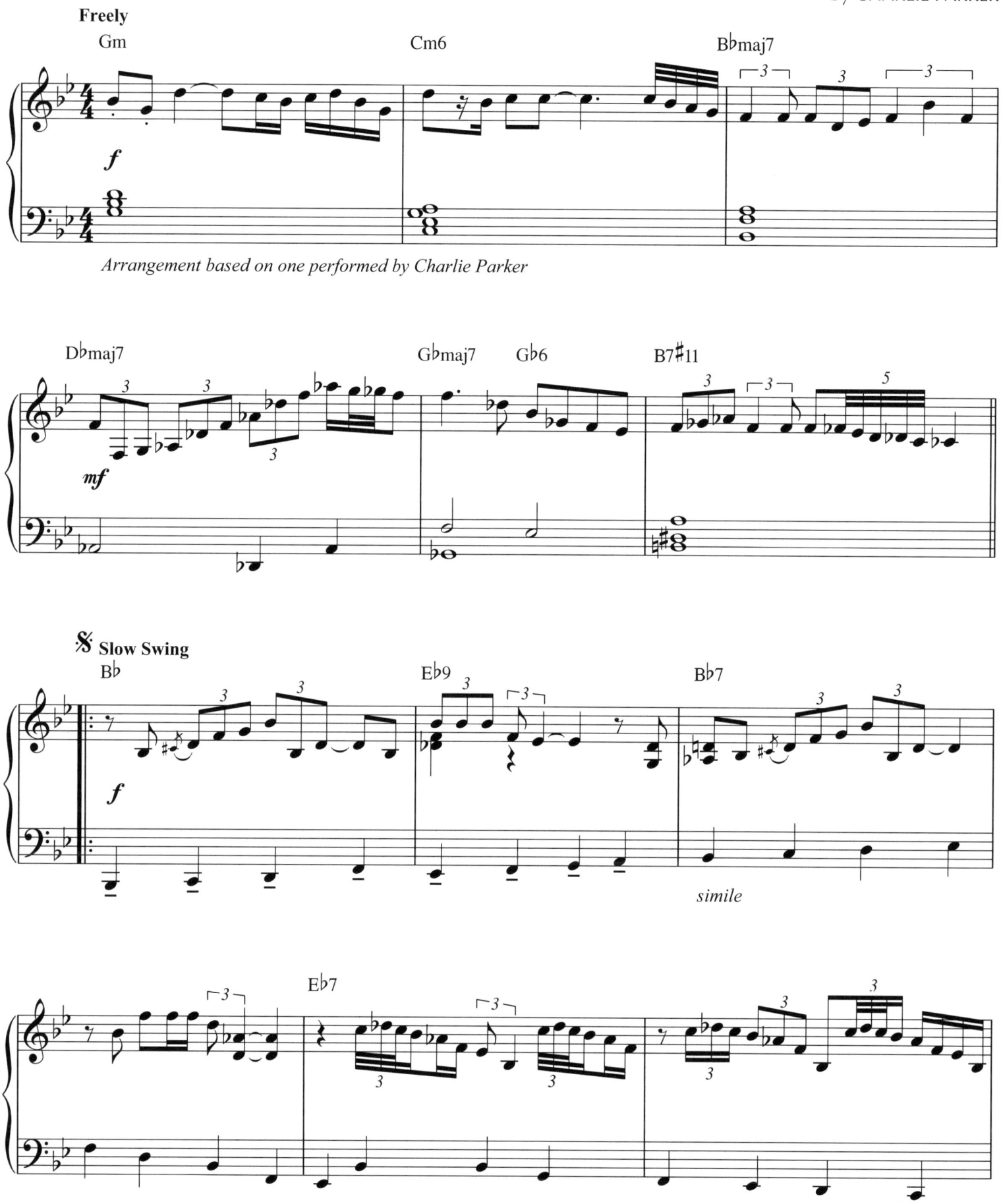


Copyright © 1948 Atlantic Music Corp.
Copyright Renewed and Assigned 1976 Atlantic Music Corp.
This arrangement Copyright © 2016 Atlantic Music Corp.
All Rights for the World excluding the U.S. Controlled and Administered by Screen Gems-EMI Music Inc.
International Copyright Secured All Rights Reserved

B♭7
Dm7
G7♭9
Cm7
F7
To Coda
B♭
Cm
1.
B♭6/F
F7
2.
F
F7♯5
B♭9
straight 8ths
E♭9
B♭7
Fm7
B♭7♯5
E♭9

Edim7
B♭
B♭/F
B♭/D
C♯m7
F♯7/C♯
Cm7
F7
Cm7
F7
B♭7
E♭7
Edim7
B♭/F
D.S. al Coda
CODA
Freely
B♭/F
F7♯5
Gm
Cm6
B♭6
D♭7
G♭maj7
B13♯11
pp

# RELAXIN' AT THE CAMARILLO

By CHARLIE PARKER

Copyright © 1961 SONGS OF UNIVERSAL, INC.
Copyright Renewed
This arrangement Copyright © 2016 SONGS OF UNIVERSAL, INC.
All Rights Reserved Used by Permission

Gm7
G♭7
F6
F7
C
Dm7
Em7
A7♭9
Dm7
G7
Dm7
G7
C
To Coda
Dm9
G7
C
F9
Solo based on ones by Charlie Parker
and Dodo Marmarosa
C
Gm7
C7
F7

F9
Cmaj9
Dm7
Em7
A7
Dm7
G7
3
3
C
A7
Dm7
G7
C
F6
3
Fm
C
G♭7♯11
F6
Fm7
B♭7
Cmaj7
B♭13

A7♭9
Dm11
G7
Em7
Am7
Dm7
G7
C13
f
D♭7
C7
D♭7
C7
C7♭5(♭9)
F7♯11
C
Dm7
straight 8ths
Em7
E♭m7
Dm7
D7
G7
D♭7

D.S. al Coda
C7
B♭7
A7sus
Dm7
G7♭5(♭9)
CODA
C
Cmaj7
B♭maj7
A♭maj7
G♭maj7
Emaj7
E♭m7
D♭maj7
Cmaj7
f
8vb
Cmaj7
B♭maj7
A♭maj7
G♭maj7
Emaj7
E♭m7
(8vb)
D♭maj7
Cmaj7
8vb

# SCRAPPLE FROM THE APPLE

By CHARLIE PARKER

Copyright © 1957 (Renewed 1985) Atlantic Music Corp.
This arrangement Copyright © 2016 Atlantic Music Corp.
International Copyright Secured All Rights Reserved

F
B♭6
Bdim7
F/C
Gm7
1.
Am7
D7
2.
F
Em7
f
A9
D9sus
D7
G7
Dm11
G7
C7
Gm7
C7♭5
Gm7
mf
C7

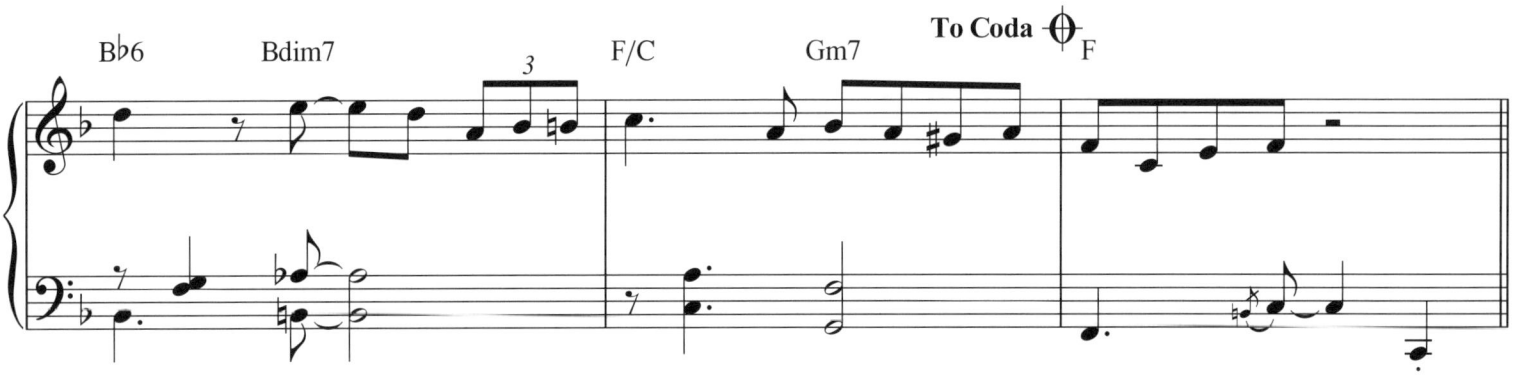


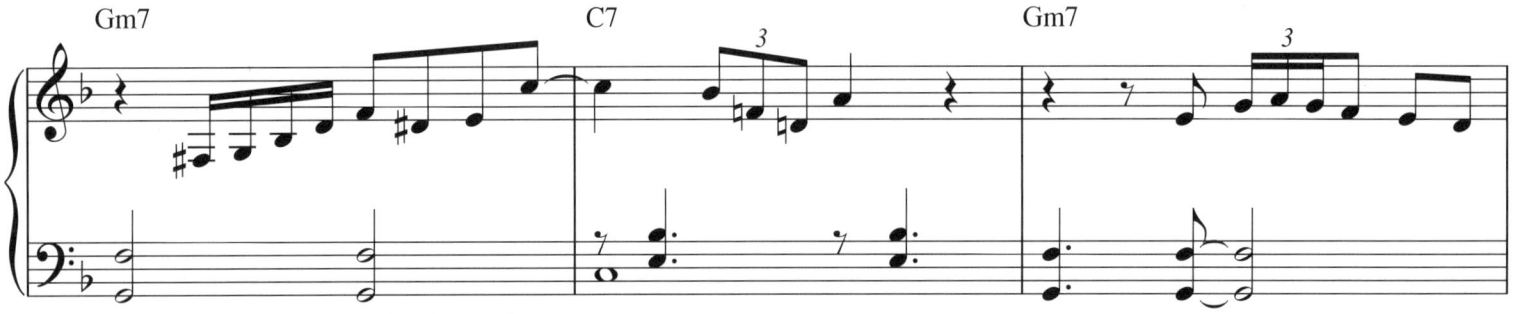


*Solo based on one by Charlie Parker*

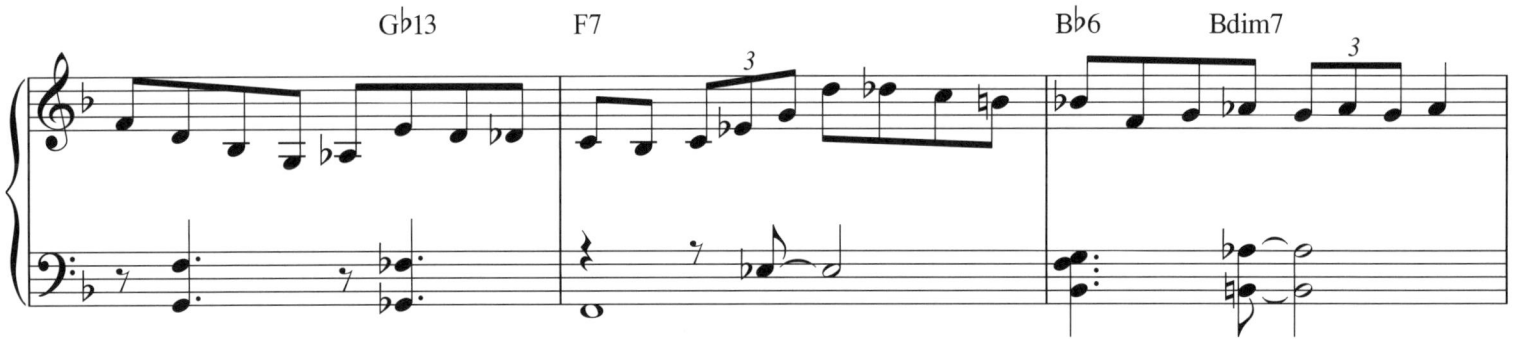


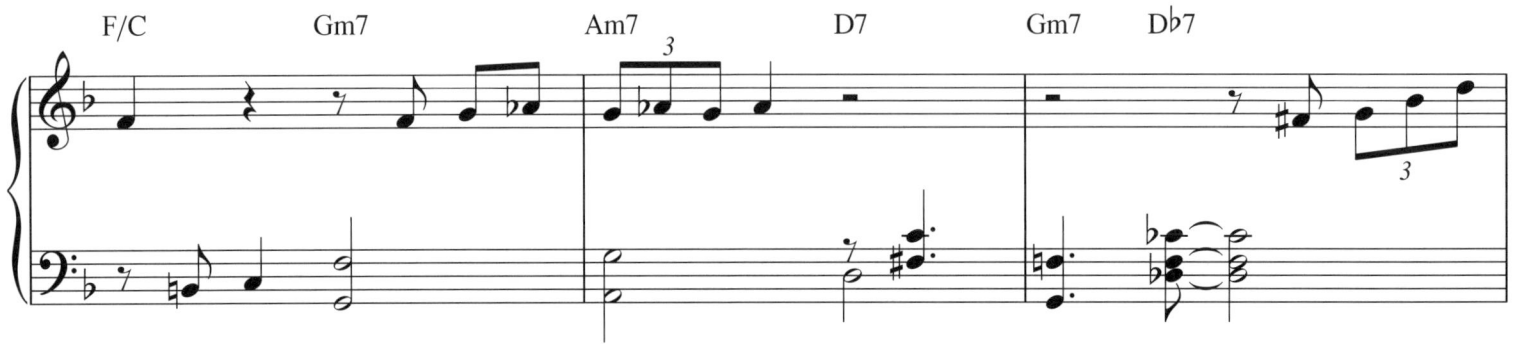

C7
Gm7♭5
D♭7
C7
F6
Gm7
A♭dim7
F/C
G♭6/9
F6
Am7
Em7
A7
D7
f
Am11
D7
G7
Gm7
D♭7♯11
C7
Gm7
mf

C7
F♯7
Gm7
D♭7
C7♯5

F6
Gm7
C7
F/C

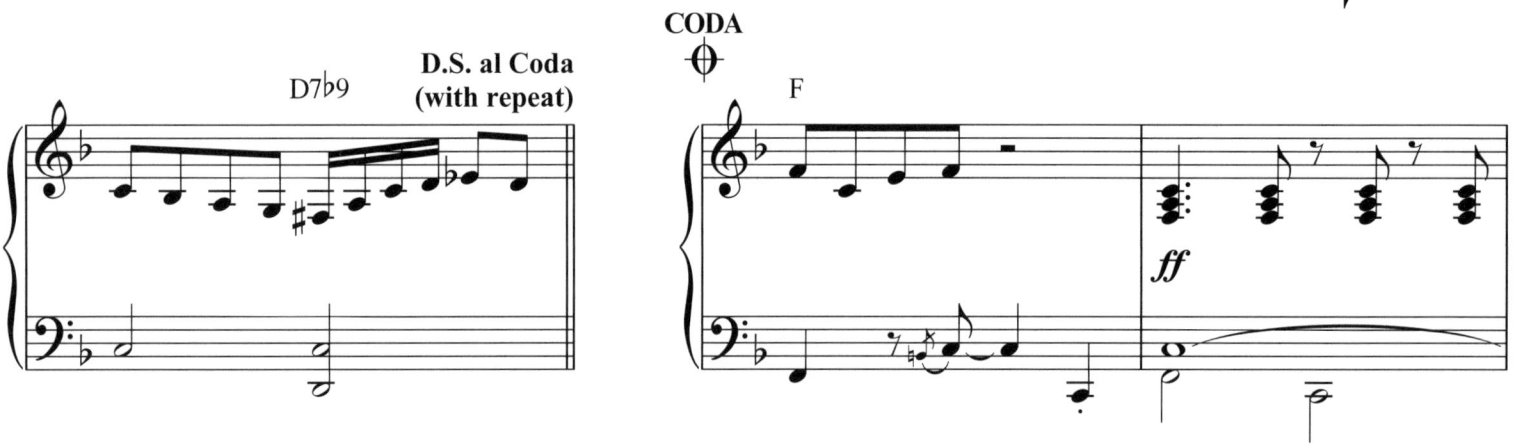
D7♭9
D.S. al Coda
(with repeat)
CODA
F
ff

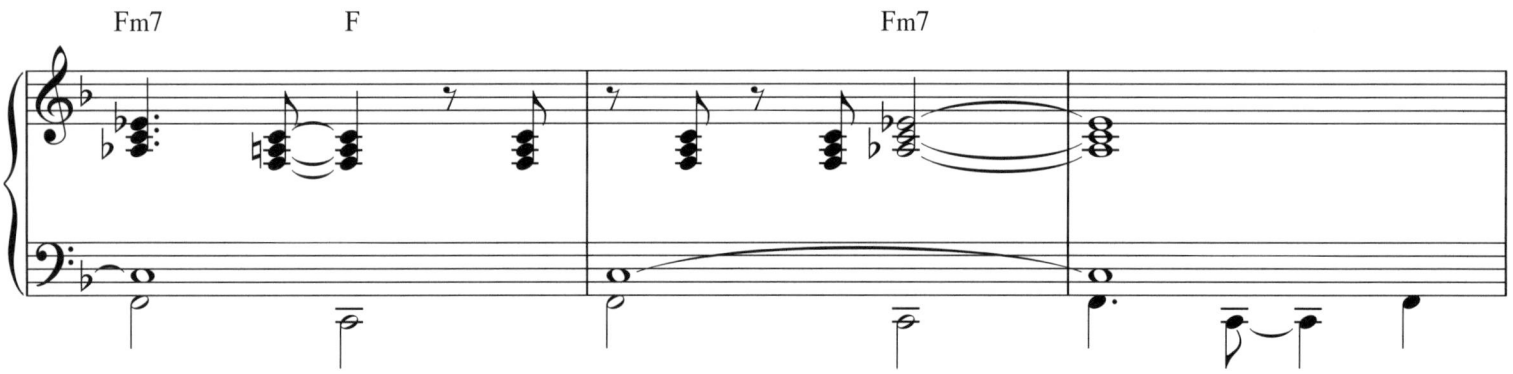
Fm7
F
Fm7

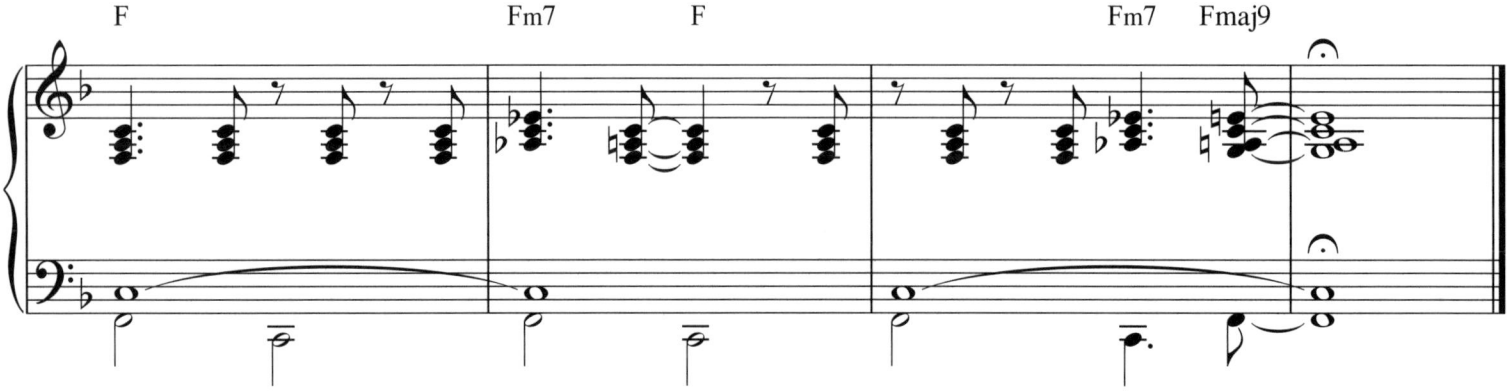
F
Fm7
F
Fm7
Fmaj9

# SUMMERTIME

## from PORGY AND BESS®

Music and Lyrics by GEORGE GERSHWIN,
DuBOSE and DOROTHY HEYWARD
and IRA GERSHWIN

© 1935 (Renewed) NOKAWI MUSIC, FRANKIE G. SONGS, DUBOSE AND DOROTHY HEYWARD MEMORIAL FUND PUBLISHING and IRA GERSHWIN MUSIC
This arrangement © 2016 NOKAWI MUSIC, FRANKIE G. SONGS, DUBOSE AND DOROTHY HEYWARD MEMORIAL FUND PUBLISHING and IRA GERSHWIN MUSIC
All Rights for NOKAWI MUSIC Administered by IMAGEM SOUNDS
All Rights for FRANKIE G. SONGS and DUBOSE AND DOROTHY HEYWARD MEMORIAL FUND PUBLISHING Administered by SONGS MUSIC PUBLISHING
All Rights for IRA GERSHWIN MUSIC Administered by WB MUSIC CORP.
All Rights Reserved Used by Permission

Swing 8ths
D7
Gm6
D7/A
Gm6
D7/A
mf
Gm6
D7/A
Gm
C7♯11
B♭/F
Gm
f
C9♯11
F9
Gm
C9/G
Gm6
Straight 8ths
D9♯5
Gm6
D7/A
Gm6
D7
mf
Gm6/B♭
D7/A
Gm/B♭
D7
Gm6
Cm7
Cm7/E♭

Cm7/G
E♭7
D7
A7♯9
D7♭9
f
Swing 8ths
Gm6
D9/A
Gm6
D7/A
Gm6
D7/A
Gm6
C7♯11
mf
Freely
B♭/F
Gm
D7♯5(♭9)
f
Gm6
C
F9sus
B♭6
E♭7
mf a tempo
A♭maj7
D13♭9
Gm6
Straight 8ths
f
mp

# YARDBIRD SUITE

By CHARLIE PARKER

Copyright © 1946 ATLANTIC MUSIC CORP.
Copyright Renewed
This arrangement Copyright © 2016 ATLANTIC MUSIC CORP.
All Rights Reserved Used by Permission

1.
D9
G9sus
G9
Em7
A7
Dm7
G7
2.
G9sus
C6
F♯m7♭5
B7
Em6
F♯m7♭5
B7♭9
f
Em
A9
A7♭9
Dm
Em7
A7♯5
D9
G7
D♭9♯11
G7♯5

C6/9
Fm11
B♭9
C6/9
B♭13
A9
mf
To Coda
D9
G9
D♭maj13
C6
G7♭9
C
Solo based on one by Charlie Parker
Fm11
B♭7sus
C6
B♭7
A7♭9
D9
Dm7
G7
Em
Am7

Dm11
G13
C6
Fm11
B♭9sus
C7
A7♭9
D9
G9
C
C7
B7
Em
F♯m11♭5
B7
f
Em
A9
A7♭9
Dm
3
3

Em7♭5
A9
D13
A♭7♯5(♭9)
G9sus
D♭7
C6
Fm11
B♭7
C7
B♭7
A13
D13
Dm7
G7sus
C6/9
A7♭9
Dm7
G13sus
D.S. al Coda
CODA
Dm7
G7
Cmaj9
ff